FOOD LOVERS

BABY AND
TODDLER

RECIPES SELECTED BY JONNIE LÉGER

Trans
Atlantic
Press

All recipes make four servings, unless otherwise indicated.

The recipes in this book range from simple puréed fruits and vegetables to meals that can be shared by the whole family. ALWAYS consult your doctor or health visitor before introducing new foods to your baby and carefully follow their guidelines about weaning and feeding babies and young children.

For best results when cooking the recipes in this book, buy fresh ingredients and follow the instructions carefully. Make sure that everything is properly cooked through before serving, particularly any meat and shellfish, and note that as a general rule vulnerable groups such as the very young, elderly people, pregnant women, convalescents and anyone suffering from an illness should avoid dishes that contain raw or lightly cooked eggs.

For all recipes, quantities are given in metric measurements followed by the equivalent in standard U.S. cups and imperial measures. Follow one set or the other, but not a mixture of both because conversions may not be exact. Standard spoon and cup measurements are level and are based on the following:

1 tsp. = 5 ml, 1 tbsp. = 15 ml, 1 cup = 250 ml / 8 fl oz.

Note that Australian standard tablespoons are 20 ml, so Australian readers should use 3 tsp. in place of 1 tbsp. when measuring small quantities.

The electric oven temperatures in this book are given for conventional ovens with top and bottom heat. The cooking times given should be used as an approximate guideline only.

CONTENTS

RED LENTIL, CARROT AND TOMATO PURÉE

Ingredients

2 tsp olive oil

½ small onion, chopped

1 large carrot, scrubbed and chopped

75 g / ⅓ cup red lentils

1 tsp tomato paste

Method

Prep and cook time: 1 hour

1 Heat the oil in a large skillet (frying pan), add the onion and cook gently for 5 minutes, until softened but not browned. Add the carrot and continue cooking for another 4–5 minutes.

2 Add the lentils, tomato paste and 475 ml / 2 cups of water. Bring to a boil, reduce heat and simmer for 40–50 minutes, or until the lentils are soft.

3 Drain the mixture, reserving the liquid. Purée the solids in a food processor or blender until smooth, adding the leftover liquid 1 tbsp at a time until the desired consistency is reached. Serve at room temperature.

SWEET POTATO PURÉE

Ingredients

1 small sweet potato

Method

Prep and cook time: 50 min

1 Heat the oven to 200C (400F / Gas Mark 6).

2 Pierce the sweet potato several times with a fork and place on a baking sheet. Bake until tender, about 40 minutes.

3 Scoop the potato flesh from the skin and put into a bowl, adding 2 tbsp of hot water. Mash with a fork or stick (immersion) blender to make a smooth consistency, adding more water if needed.

BUTTERNUT SQUASH PURÉE

Ingredients

150 g / 5 oz (¼ medium) butternut squash, halved and seeded

Method

Prep and cook time: 50 min

1 Heat the oven to 200C (400F / Gas Mark 6).

2 Place the squash, flesh side down, in an ovenproof dish with 5 tbsp water. Bake until tender, about 40 minutes.

3 Scoop the flesh from the skin and put into a bowl, adding 2 tbsp of hot water or squash cooking liquid. Mash with a fork or stick (immersion) blender to make a smooth consistency, adding more water if needed.

APPLE PURÉE

Ingredients

225 g / 8 oz cooking apple, peeled, cored and sliced

25 g / 2 tbsp superfine (caster) sugar

Apple slices, to garnish

Method

Prep and cook time: 15 min

1 Put the apples into a heatproof bowl with the sugar and 2 tbsp water.

2 Cover with microwave-safe plastic wrap (clingfilm), pierce a few times and cook on High for 4 minutes until soft. Let stand for 2 minutes. Or put all the ingredients in a pan and heat gently until the apples are soft.

3 Using a stick (immersion) blender, blend the apples to a smooth purée. Garnish with apple slices.

BANANA CHOCOLATE FROMAGE BLANC

Ingredients

2 tablespoons chocolate chips

2 ripe bananas

4 tbsp fromage blanc (frais)

To garnish:

Banana slices

Cocoa powder

Method

Prep and cook time: 10 min

1 In a medium microwave-safe bowl, microwave the chocolate chips on medium power, stirring every 20 seconds, just until melted.

2 Slice the bananas directly into the bowl and mash well with a fork until smoothly blended into the chocolate. Stir in the fromage blanc (frais).

3 Garnish with sliced banana and sprinkle with cocoa powder.

CARROT SOUP

Ingredients

1 tbsp olive oil

1 small onion, chopped

900 ml / 4 cups boiling water

500 g / 1 lb carrots, roughly chopped

2 tsp honey

To garnish:

2 tbsp plain dried breadcrumbs

1 tsp chopped fresh dill, if desired

Method

Prep and cook time: 30 min

1 Heat the oil in a large, heavy pot or Dutch oven. Add the onion and fry gently for 5 minutes until softened but not browned.

2 Add the boiling water, carrots and honey. Cover and simmer for 20 minutes until the carrots are tender.

3 Remove from the heat. Use a stick (immersion) blender to blend the mixture to a semi-smooth purée (or transfer to a blender or food processor). If you know your child prefers it lump-free, continue blending until the soup is really smooth.

4 Serve at room temperature, garnished with a sprinkling of breadcrumbs and dill.

SWEET POTATO AND SQUASH SOUP WITH CHICKEN

Ingredients

2 tomatoes

2 tsp olive oil

1 small onion, chopped

800 ml / 3½ cups vegetable broth (stock) or water

300 g / 12 oz butternut squash, peeled, seeded, and chopped

1 medium sweet potato, peeled and roughly chopped

1 skinless, boneless chicken breast, chopped

Method

Prep and cook time: 40 min

1 Bring a medium saucepan of water to a boil; drop in the tomatoes and heat for 1–3 minutes until the tomato skins split. Remove the tomatoes with a slotted spoon; when cool enough to handle, peel and coarsely chop.

2 Heat the oil in a large saucepan or soup pot; add the onion and fry for a few minutes to soften (do not brown).

3 Add the broth (stock) or water, squash, sweet potato, tomatoes and chicken. Cover and simmer for 15 minutes until the vegetables are soft.

4 Remove a ladleful of the vegetables and reserve. Use a stick (immersion) blender to whiz the rest of the soup to a smooth purée (or transfer in batches to a blender or food processor). Return the reserved vegetables to the soup and serve.

COTTAGE PIE

Ingredients

1 tbsp vegetable oil

2 onions, chopped

450 g / 1 lb ground beef

450 ml / 2 cups beef broth (stock)

1 tbsp all-purpose flour

1 tbsp Worcestershire sauce

1 tbsp tomato purée

Salt and freshly ground pepper, to taste

900 g / 2 lb potatoes, peeled and cut into chunks

25 g / 2 tbsp butter

4 tbsp milk

Method

Prep and cook time: 1 hour 30 min

1 Heat the oven to 170C (325F / Gas Mark 3).

2 Heat the oil in a large flameproof casserole and fry the onions for 5 minutes until softened.

3 Add the beef and cook, stirring, until well browned. Stir in the broth (stock), flour, Worcestershire sauce and tomato purée. Bring to a boil and season with salt and pepper. Cover and carefully transfer to the oven. Bake for 20 minutes, until tender.

4 Meanwhile, put the potatoes into a saucepan with enough salted water to cover. Bring to a boil, reduce the heat and simmer for 20–25 minutes until very tender.

5 Drain the potatoes, return to the pan, and mash until very smooth. Beat in the butter and milk.

6 Increase the oven temperature to 220C (400F / Gas Mark 6).

7 Spoon the beef into a 1.7 liter / 1½-quart baking dish. Spread the potato mixture on top, to completely cover the meat. Place on a baking sheet and bake for 25 minutes or until the top is starting to brown.

RATATOUILLE WITH RICE

Ingredients

2 tbsp olive oil

1 onion, chopped

225 g / 8 oz zucchini (courgette, chopped

175 g / 6 oz eggplant (aubergine), chopped

1 clove garlic, crushed

400 g / 14 oz can chopped tomatoes

1 tbsp tomato paste

100 g / ½ cup long-grain rice

Method

Prep and cook time: 1 hour

1 Heat the oil in a large skillet. Add the onion and cook gently for 5 minutes to soften (do not brown). Add the zucchini (courgette), eggplant (aubergine) and garlic; fry for a few minutes.

2 Stir in the tomatoes and tomato paste; cover and simmer for 20 minutes until the vegetables are tender.

3 Meanwhile, put the rice into a pan with 225ml / 1 cup cold salted water. Cover and bring to a boil; reduce the heat and simmer for 15 minutes until the rice is tender and the liquid is absorbed.

4 Serve the ratatouille with the rice.

FISH PIE

Ingredients

800 g / 2 lb starchy potato, peeled and cut into chunks

250 g / 8 oz skinless white fish fillet

250 g / 8 oz skinless smoked haddock fillet

1 small onion, quartered

600 ml / 2½ cups full-fat milk, divided

200 g / 8 oz frozen green peas

100 g / 7 tablespoons butter, divided

50 g / ½ cup all-purpose (plain) flour

Salt and freshly ground pepper, to taste

Pinch freshly grated nutmeg

Method

Prep and cook time: 1 hour

1 Put the potatoes into a large pan of salted water and bring to a boil. Reduce heat and simmer for 20 minutes until tender.

2 Meanwhile, arrange the white fish, smoked haddock and onion in a large skillet; add 475ml / 2 cups of the milk. Bring the milk just to a boil – you will see a few small bubbles. Reduce the heat and simmer for 8 minutes; set aside.

3 Lift the fish into an ovenproof dish. Retain the cooking liquid and discard the onion. Flake the fish into large pieces in the baking dish. Scatter the frozen peas over the fish.

4 To make the sauce, melt 3 tablespoons of the butter in a saucepan; stir in the flour and cook for 1 minute over a moderate heat. Gradually pour in a little of the retained poaching milk, then stir until blended. Continue to add the rest of the milk gradually, mixing well until you have a smooth thickened sauce. Remove from the heat, season with salt, pepper and nutmeg, then pour over the fish.

5 Heat the oven to 200C (400F / Gas Mark 8).

6 Drain the potatoes and return to the pan with the remaining butter and milk. Season to taste and mash until smooth and lump free. Spoon the mashed potato all over the fish. Fluff the top with a fork.

7 Bake for 30 minutes until the top is golden.

PASTA SALAD
WITH STRAWBERRIES

Ingredients

150 g / 5 oz (2 cups) fusilli

1 tbsp olive oil

2 tsp lemon juice

50 g / $\frac{1}{3}$ cup crumbled feta or ricotta cheese

200 g / 1½ cups strawberries, hulled and quartered

Mint leaves, torn

Method

Prep and cook time: 15 min

1 Bring a large pot of salted water to a boil and add the pasta. Cook according to the package instructions, until al dente. Drain in a colander under cold running water. Transfer to a large bowl.

2 Pour over the oil and lemon juice and toss to coat.

3 Divide into 4 serving bowls. Crumble over the cheese, scatter over the strawberries and mint leaves and serve within a couple of hours.

MINI PIZZAS

Ingredients
For 12 mini pizzas

For the pizza base:

400 g / 4 cups all-purpose (plain) flour

20 g / ¾ oz dried yeast

1 tsp. sugar

1 tsp. salt

240 ml / 1 cup lukewarm water

For the pizza topping:

5 tbsp. olive oil

600 g / 3 cups tomato sauce (passata)

Salt and freshly milled pepper

100 g / 4 oz finely sliced ham or prosciutto

½ a red onion, chopped

200 g / 7 oz mozzarella cheese

2 scallions (spring onion), sliced

Method
Prep and cook time: 45 min plus raising time 1 h 40 min

1 For the pizza base, mix together the flour, yeast, sugar, salt and the lukewarm water. Knead to form a smooth dough, then cover and put in a warm place for about 1 hour to rise. Knead the dough again, cover and leave for 30–40 minutes to rise again.

2 Line a cookie sheet with parchment paper. Divide the pizza dough into 12 balls. Roll out each ball on a floured surface. Place on the cookie sheet and press flat, leaving the edge slightly thicker.

3 Pre-heat the oven to 425°F (220°C / Gas Mark 7). Brush each pizza base with a little of the olive oil, then spread tomato sauce (passata) over the top. Season with salt and pepper.

4 Scatter the ham, onion and scallions (spring onions) over the mini-pizzas and sprinkle the cheese over the top. Bake in the oven for about 8–12 minutes until golden brown.

FISH CRUMBLE

Ingredients

450 g / 1 lb fish fillet, cut
into chunks (or tuna chunks if
preferred)

100 g / 4 oz medium shrimp
(prawns)

250 g / 8 oz mascarpone

1 lemon

For the crumble:

125 g / 1 cup all-purpose
(plain) flour

75 g / 5 tbsp butter,
cubed

1 tbsp chopped parsley

Method

Prep and cook time: 55 min

1 Heat the oven to 190C (375F / Gas Mark 5). Grease a
large baking dish.

2 Arrange the fish and shrimp (prawns) in the dish.

3 Combine the mascarpone with 4 tbsp of cold water
and the finely grated zest and juice of the lemon, to taste.
Spoon the mascarpone mixture over the fish.

4 Put the flour, butter and parsley together in a food
processor, or bowl. Pulse together in the processor, or
rub together with your fingertips until the mixture forms
crumbs.

5 Sprinkle the crumble mixture evenly over the fish. Bake
for 35 minutes, until the crumble is golden.

MACARONI CHEESE WITH HAM

Ingredients

225 g / 8 oz stubby macaroni, such as penne, elbows or fusilli

50 g / 4 tablespoons butter

50 g / ½ cup all-purpose (plain) flour

900 ml / 4 cups milk

225 g / 8 oz Emmental cheese, grated

100 g / 3½ oz wafer-thin ham slices, chopped

½ tsp freshly grated nutmeg

Method

Prep and cook time: 25 min

1 Heat the broiler (grill).

2 Bring a large pot of salted water to a boil and add the pasta. Cook according to the package instructions, until al dente.

3 Meanwhile, melt the butter in a medium nonstick skillet (frying pan). Add the flour and cook, stirring, for 1 minute. Gradually add the milk, whisking all the time to make a smooth sauce. Keep stirring until the sauce is thickened.

4 Drain the macaroni and add to the sauce with the cheese, ham and nutmeg.

5 Pour into an ovenproof dish and broil (grill) for 2–3 minutes, just until top is browned, then serve.

SPAGHETTI BOLOGNESE

Ingredients

250 g / 8 oz lean ground (minced) beef

1 tbsp olive oil

1 onion, chopped

1 carrot, chopped

1 roasted red bell pepper, drained

400 g / 14 oz can plum tomatoes, drained

2 dashes Worcestershire sauce

200 g / 7 oz spaghetti

To garnish:

Basil leaves

Method

Prep and cook time: 40 min

1 Fry the beef in a large nonstick skillet for 15 minutes, until browned.

2 Meanwhile, heat the oil in a large skillet, add the onion and carrot; cook for 5 minutes to soften.

3 Chop the bell pepper and add it to the carrot and onion. Stir in the tomatoes and their juice, and cook for 5 minutes more.

4 Purée the tomato mixture in a blender or food processor until smooth.

5 Add the tomato sauce and Worcestershire sauce to the beef. Add 100 ml / ½ cup of water, stir, cover and simmer for 10 minutes.

6 Meanwhile, bring a large pot of salted water to a boil, add the spaghetti and cook according to package instructions, for about 10 minutes, until al dente.

7 Drain the pasta and divide between 4 plates. Top with the beef mixture and garnish with basil leaves.

BREADED FISH FINGERS

Ingredients

100 g / 1½ cups fresh breadcrumbs

1 tbsp chopped fresh parsley

2 tbsp mayonnaise

3 tbsp all-purpose flour

2 eggs, beaten

450 g / 1 lb skinless cod fillets, cut into finger-size strips

Green peas, to serve

Method

Prep and cook time: 30 min

1 Heat the oven to 220C (400F / Gas Mark 7).

2 Mix the breadcrumbs, parsley and mayonnaise together in a bowl until combined.

3 Place the breadcrumb mixture, flour and beaten egg in 3 separate shallow bowls. Coat each piece of fish first in the flour, shaking off the excess, then dip into the egg and finally, roll in the breadcrumbs.

4 Place the fish fingers on a nonstick baking sheet and bake for 8–10 minutes, until lightly golden and crisp.

5 Meanwhile, cook the peas according to the package directions, and serve with the fish.

BAKED BROCCOLI RISOTTO

Ingredients

25 g / 2 tbsp butter

1 onion, chopped

300 g / 12 oz risotto rice

150 g / ½ cup broccoli, cut into small florets

700 ml / 3 cups hot vegetable broth (stock)

50 g / ½ cup Cheddar cheese, grated

25 g / 1 oz plain dry breadcrumbs

Method

Prep and cook time: 35 min

1 Heat the oven to 200C (400F / Gas Mark 6).

2 Heat the butter in a flameproof casserole. Add the onion and cook, stirring, for 3–4 minutes until softened but not browned.

3 Add the rice and mix well until coated. Add the broccoli and the hot broth (stock), then give the rice a quick stir.

4 Cover with a tightly fitting lid and bake for 15 minutes until just cooked.

5 Stir in the cheese and sprinkle with the breadcrumbs. Return to the oven for a few minutes until crumb topping is golden.

PASTA WITH SPINACH, TOMATOES AND CHICKEN

Ingredients

200 g / 8 oz stubby macaroni, such as penne or rigatoni

1 tbsp olive oil

1 skinless, boneless chicken breast, cubed

125 ml / ½ cup milk

125 ml / ½ cup light cream

150 g / ½ cup thawed frozen spinach

2 tbsp instant flour (thickening granules)

1 tbsp grated Parmesan cheese

Salt and freshly ground pepper, to taste

8 cherry tomatoes, halved

To garnish:

4 basil leaves

Method

Prep and cook time: 30 min

1 Bring a large pan of salted water to a boil. Add the pasta and cook according to package instructions, until al dente.

2 Meanwhile, heat the oil in a large skillet. Add the chicken and fry, turning as needed, until cooked through, 10 minutes.

3 Combine the milk, cream and spinach in a medium saucepan; stir in the instant flour (thickening granules), bring to a boil and simmer, stirring, until thickened. Stir in the Parmesan cheese and season with salt and pepper.

4 Drain the macaroni and add to the creamy sauce with the chicken and tomatoes.

5 Serve the pasta in bowls garnished with basil leaves.

APPLE MUFFINS

Ingredients

For 12 muffins

225 g / 2 cups all-purpose flour

75 g / $^1/_3$ cup superfine (caster) sugar

2 tsp baking soda (bicarbonate of soda)

1 tsp cinnamon, divided

150 ml / $^2/_3$ cup milk

50 ml / ¼ cup sunflower oil

1 egg

2 apples, peeled, cored and finely chopped

50 g / ¼ cup light brown sugar

Method

Prep and cook time: 35 min

1 Heat the oven to 190C (375F / Gas Mark 5). Line a 12-cup muffin tin with paper liners.

2 Combine the flour, sugar, baking soda (bicarbonate of soda) and ½ tsp of the cinnamon in a large bowl. Add the milk, oil, egg and apples; stir for a few seconds until just combined. Spoon the mixture into the prepared muffin cups.

3 Mix the brown sugar and the remaining ½ tsp cinnamon. Sprinkle over each muffin.

4 Bake for 15–20 minutes until firm and lightly browned.

RICE PUDDING
WITH BERRIES

Ingredients

For the baked rice pudding:

75 g / scant ½ cup short-grain rice

600 ml / 2½ cups milk

25 g / 2 tbsp superfine (caster) sugar

For the summer berries:

300 g / 12 oz mixed frozen
summer berries, such as raspberries,
redcurrants and blueberries

50 g / ¼ cup superfine (caster) sugar

Method
Prep and cook time: 1 hour

1 Heat the oven to 170C (325F / Gas Mark 3).
Grease a 900 ml / 1-quart baking dish.

2 Add the rice, milk and sugar. Cover with foil and
bake for 1 hour until the rice is tender.

3 Meanwhile, put the frozen berries into a saucepan
with the sugar and 3 tbsp water. Heat for 5 minutes
until the fruit is tender and the sugar is dissolved.

4 To serve, add the rice pudding to the warm
summer berries.

BAKED BANANAS
WITH ORANGE
AND COCONUT

Ingredients

4 tsp firmly packed brown sugar

4 tsp butter

2 bananas

1 orange

4 tsp shredded dried coconut

Method

Prep and cook time: 25 min

1 Heat the oven to 350F (180C / Gas Mark 4). Cut 4 x 20-cm / 8-inch squares of foil.

2 Put 1 tsp of sugar in the center of each foil piece, along with 1 tsp butter.

3 Slice the bananas and scatter on top of the butter and sugar mixture.

4 Use a serrated knife to cut away the orange peel and pith. Cut the orange segments away from the orange membrane, catching the juice. Scatter the orange segments over the bananas with the coconut.

5 Gather up the foil edges and pour over any reserved orange juice. Seal each parcel and place on a baking sheet. Bake for 15 minutes to warm through.

FRENCH TOAST WITH BANANA

Ingredients

150 ml / $2/3$ cup milk

3 eggs

2 tbsp butter

8 slices whole-wheat bread, shaped into stars with a cutter

3 tbsp caster (superfine) sugar

To garnish:

1 banana

Fresh lemon juice

Method

Prep and cook time: 20 min

1 Put the milk and eggs into a shallow bowl, and beat together with a fork.

2 Heat the butter in a large nonstick skillet (frying pan).

3 Working quickly, dip the bread "stars" into the egg mixture, lift out and place in the skillet. Fry for a couple minutes, then turn them over and cook for another couple of minutes until golden.

4 Sprinkle the French toast with sugar.

5 Arrange 2 stars on each plate. Slice the banana, toss in the lemon juice and garnish the French toast with a few slices of banana.

RASPBERRY FROZEN YOGURT

Ingredients

50 g / scant $^1/_3$ cup sifted icing (confectioners') sugar

300 g / 12 oz frozen raspberries

4 tbsp honey

500 g / 1 lb low fat plain yogurt

To garnish:

12 raspberries

Method

Prep and cook time: 20 min plus at least 5 hours freezing time and 20 min defrosting time

1 Put the confectioners' sugar into a food processor with the raspberries and whiz together until smooth, or mash everything together with a potato masher.

2 Add the honey and yogurt and whiz together to combine, or mix with a potato masher. Do not overprocess.

3 Spoon into a freezer-proof container, seal and freeze for several hours.

4 To serve, remove the frozen yogurt from the freezer for 20 minutes to soften slightly. Serve garnished with fresh raspberries.

PANCAKES WITH RASPBERRIES
AND MAPLE SYRUP

Ingredients

125 g / 1 cup + 2 tbsp all-purpose flour

2 eggs

200 ml / ¾ cup + 2 tbsp milk

2 tbsp vegetable oil

200 g / 1 cup raspberries

4 tbsp maple syrup

Method

Prep and cook time: 20 min

1 Put the flour in a bowl, then gradually whisk in the eggs and milk until smooth. (This can also be done in a food processor.)

2 Heat a thin layer of oil in a nonstick skillet or griddle until a drop of water skitters when dripped on the surface. Add 3 tbsp of the batter to the pan, swirling to coat the base of the pan.

3 Cook the pancake for 2 minutes until firm and golden brown underneath, then use a nonstick spatula to flip the pancake over. Cook for 1minute more.

4 Slide the pancake onto a warm plate. Continue with the rest of the batter, stacking the finished pancakes between sheets of wax paper, so they don't stick together.

5 Use a flower or star-shaped cutter to stamp out shaped pancakes, if desired. Serve with raspberries, drizzled with maple syrup.

Published by Transatlantic Press

First published in 2011

Transatlantic Press
38 Copthorne Road, Croxley Green, Hertfordshire WD3 4AQ

© Transatlantic Press

Images and Recipes by StockFood © The Food Image Agency

Recipes selected by Jonnie Léger, StockFood

A catalogue record for this book is available from the British Library.

ISBN 978-1-908533-67-8

Printed in China